Wow! Vehicles

A Book of Extraordinary Facts

KINGFISHER

First published 2018 by Kingfisher
an imprint of Macmillan Children's Books
20 New Wharf Road, London N1 9RR
Associated companies throughout the world
www.panmacmillan.com

Author: Jacqueline McCann
Design and styling: Liz Adcock
Cover design: Liz Adcock
Illustrations: Ste Johnson

ISBN 978-0-7534-4273-9

9 8 7 6 5 4 3 2 1
1TR/0519/WKT/UG/140WFO

A CIP catalogue record for this book is available from the British Library.

Printed in China

Wow! Vehicles

A Book of Extraordinary Facts

KINGFISHER

On the move

A vehicle moves people or things from place to place. It might have wheels – but not always.

Where could you go without cars, buses, trains and planes? How would you go to school? How would grown-ups get to work? How would astronauts travel to the Moon and back?

Let's hit the road!

Wow!

The family car is one of the most common vehicles on the planet. One hundred years ago, there were only a few thousand in the world. Today, there are more than 1.2 billion!

Jet planes criss-cross the sky, carrying people around the world.

vrrrooooom

Ready to set sail? ALL aboard!

From a tiny one-person raft, sailing along a river, to a huge ocean liner, boats are a brilliant way to carry people and goods across water.

How many?

There are more than two billion bicycles in the world. More than half of them are in China!

Can you ride a bike? So can half of all the people in the world! On every continent, people ride bicycles every day. Many city roads have cycle lanes just for bicycles!

where does this go to?

Hop on, hop off

Cities are teeming with all kinds of vehicles, taking people wherever they need to go.

Look up in a busy city and you might see a cable car. Or look down and you might see steps leading to an underground railway.

Wow!

High in the Andes mountains, in Bolivia, in South America, a cable car carries 3000 people every hour between two cities: La Paz and El Alto.

There are 156 cities in the world with underground railways. Long, narrow trains speed through dark tunnels, carrying millions of passengers around each city.

Train coming!

The London Tube is the oldest underground railway in the world. It opened in 1863. Today, it has more than 270 stations and carries more than 1 billion passengers every year.

Have you ever travelled on a double-decker bus? If you find a seat on the top deck, it's a great way to see a city! Big buses carry up to 300 passengers at a time.

ALL aboard!

For one and all

The word "bus" comes from "omnibus", a word in Latin (an ancient language!) which means "for all".

10

What's that?

TAXI

If you're in a hurry and can't wait for a train or a bus, then taxis are there to help. Stand on the kerb and wave one down. Or use a mobile phone to call one and it will come and pick you up!

Fast as a bullet

Trains are a great way to travel. They're fast, they're long and some of them don't run along train tracks!

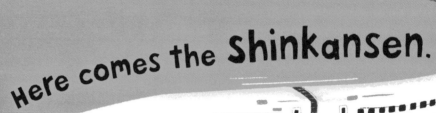

The huge network of Shinkansen trains in Japan carries millions of people around the capital, Tokyo. The Shinkansen is famous for being really fast and always on time!

Here comes the **Shinkansen.**

Watch out!

They call it **the bullet,** because it looks like one!

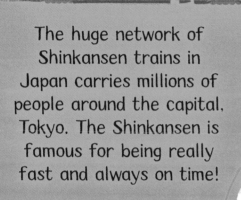

Wow!

The Trans-Siberian railway is the longest train in the world. It starts in Moscow and travels over 9300 kilometres, all the way across Russia to Vladivostok.

The magical maglev!

ALL rise ... whooooooooshhhhhh!

Maglev is short for "magnetic levitation". Do you know what that means? Instead of running along tracks, the maglev uses the power of magnets to rise and hover 10 centimetres above the tracks.
Cool!

The Maglev is the fastest train in the world. It carries 900 passengers on every trip!

Eurostar approaching ...

Neee naw, neee naw. What's that?

The Channel Tunnel is the longest undersea tunnel in the world. It connects the UK with France. Eurostar trains carry more than 10 million passengers through the tunnel every year!

9

Off to work

Lots of people do very important jobs working inside a vehicle.

An ambulance whizzes to the scene of an accident. It carries medicine and specially trained people who look after patients until they reach hospital.

Flashing light

Bandages and medicines are kept here.

Call 999!

A siren warns other vehicles to get out of the way.

Oxygen helps the patient to breathe.

Don't mess with me!

A stretcher for the patient.

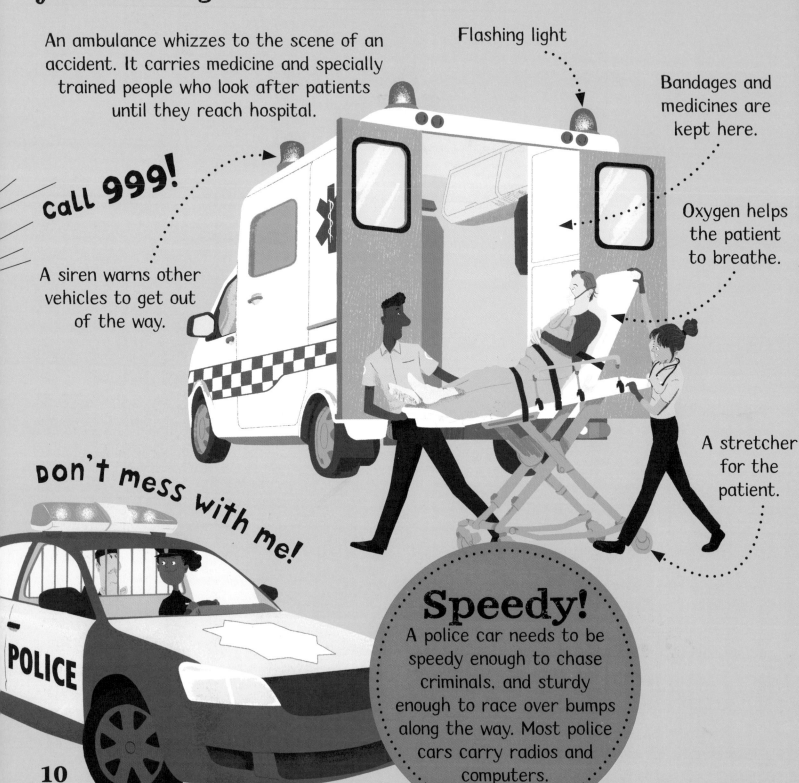

Speedy!
A police car needs to be speedy enough to chase criminals, and sturdy enough to race over bumps along the way. Most police cars carry radios and computers.

POLICE

Heavy lifting and digging are jobs for cranes and diggers. The driver uses the controls to scrape, dig and clear the ground, making it ready for homes, hospitals, schools – even sksycrapers – to be built there!

I'm a crane, lifting up!

The boom does the heavy lifting, extending like a telescope.

Wow!

The Liebherr is the most powerful mobile crane ever built. It can lift up to 1200 tonnes – that's heavier than 100 elephants!

The neck of the crane is called the jib. It bends, just like your finger.

I'm a digger, scooping down!

The excavator is like a huge bucket with teeth. It digs into the ground.

The driver of the digger sits in a cab called a house.

11

To the rescue!

A fire engine hurries to the scene of a fire, carrying firefighters and tools to put out the fire and rescue people.

A fire engine carries a huge tank of water and a long ladder that unfolds. It's the perfect vehicle to help firefighters reach the top of a tall building – and rescue any people trapped inside.

Cool!

Sometimes, summer wildfires break out in the mountains or forests. Sturdy wildland fire engines – and even planes with huge water tanks on board – race to put out the fires.

whoooooosh!

The firefighters direct a heavy stream of water onto the fire.

Long hoses spray water on the fire.

Firefighters climb up the ladder and stand on a platform at the top.

Help, I'm stuck!

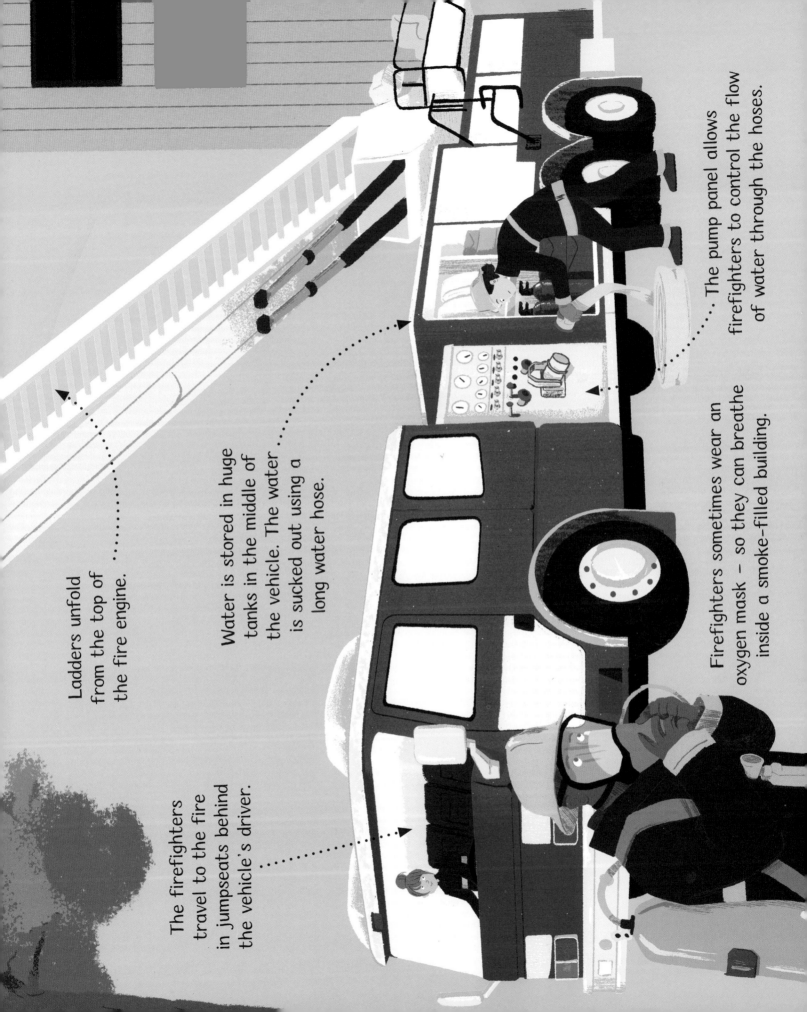

Ladders unfold from the top of the fire engine.

Water is stored in huge tanks in the middle of the vehicle. The water is sucked out using a long water hose.

The firefighters travel to the fire in jumpseats behind the vehicle's driver.

The pump panel allows firefighters to control the flow of water through the hoses.

Firefighters sometimes wear an oxygen mask – so they can breathe inside a smoke-filled building.

On the farm

There are more than seven billion people on planet Earth, and everyone needs food to eat!

Farmers do a very important job growing the food you eat. The vehicle that helps them the most is the tractor. It can pull a heavy plough to dig over a field ready for new crops – or even pull a smelly manure spreader!

The farmer sits in the cab.

Wow!

The tractor was invented in 1917, by Henry Ford (he built 15 million cars too). He realized that tractors could do more work than horses. And they eat less!

This tractor is pulling a trailer loaded with hay.

Big, fat wheels stop the heavy tractor sinking into the mud.

Tyres with deep treads grip the soil.

Once a crop has grown, the farmer needs to cut it, separate the grain from the long grass stem, then clean and bundle it. A combine harvester does everything in one go!

I'm a combine harvester.

Sheep farming

A sheep farmer needs a sturdy vehicle to pull an animal trailer. It has to drive across bumpy hills and muddy fields and have a powerful engine and big wheels with lots of grip.

Bleat, bleat!

Time for fun

Vehicles don't just do jobs for us — we use them for other important things, such as having fun!

A caravan or motorhome takes you on holiday, an ice-cream van delivers delicious cold ice cream, and a super-speedy rollercoaster will give you the ride of your life!

ALL set? Hold on tight ...

A motorhome is just what the name says — a home you motor in! It has beds and a tiny kitchen, so you can sleep and eat where you like.

It's a home on wheels!

VW

The VW Campervan is one of the world's most popular vehicles. It was first made in Germany in 1949. More than 10 million have been sold.

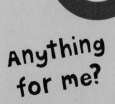

Anything for me?

Here we go ... wheeeee!

Skyscraper is a new rollercoaster in Florida, USA. When it opens in 2020 it will be the world's highest rollercoaster. It's 150 metres tall – that's higher than the London Eye ferris wheel. Awesome... and scary!

I scream, you scream, we all scream for ice cream!

Here is a vehicle most children love. The ice-cream van is brightly coloured, plays music and, best of all, helps to keep you cool on hot, sunny days, by serving ice cream!

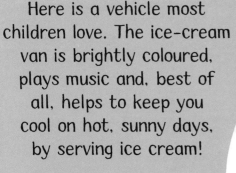

The first ice-cream van was owned by Thomas Carvellos in the USA. He had a flat tyre one day and couldn't move his van, so he decided to sell all his ice cream on the spot.

17

Vrrrooooom!

People love cars that travel fast.
The faster the better!

I'm a Vauxhall Prince Henry.

Get ready ... GO!

can you go faster?

I'm a super-cool Ferrari.

The year 1911 was the time of early car racing. The Vauxhall Prince Henry was a zippy racing car (named after a real prince) that reached a speed of 129 kilometres per hour.

Wow!

The fastest thing on two wheels is the Suzuki Hayabusa motorbike, from Japan. It zips along at 248 kilometres per hour!

By 1968, the Ferrari 365 GTS had broken all records. It went more than twice as fast as the Vauxhall Prince Henry!

Nothing is as fast on land as a supersonic car (called an SSC). In 1997, the Thrust SSC travelled at 1234 kilometres per hour. It was powered by a rocket bolted onto a jet engine!

When something travels faster than sound, it makes a noise, called a sonic boom!

BOOM!

Today, the Koenigsegg Agera (say kun-ig-segg ah-gear-ah) is the fastest car around! But you have to go to a special race called a Grand Prix to see one.

slow down!

I'm a Koenigsegg. Try and say that!

Ship ahoy

When people cross lakes, rivers and seas, wheels are no use. They need boats!

All around the world, people depend on seas and oceans for work and for food. They use all kinds of boats to catch fish.

I'm dug out of wood!

For thousands of years, people have paddled in small dugout boats, made of wood. They're a good way to go fishing!

In parts of Asia, by the coast, people meet on their boats every day at floating markets, to buy and sell food.

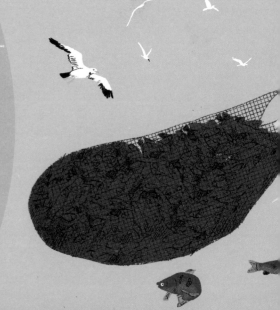

I'm a supertanker. I'm an ocean beast!

Wow!

Giant supertankers sail all over the world, carrying oil and gas. The biggest one ever built was called the *Seawise Giant*. It was over 458 metres long – that's longer than four football pitches!

Modern sailing boats have huge sails to catch the wind. Their sleek shape helps them to slice through water at high speed.

I trawl the sea for fish.

Do you like fish? Fishing boats called trawlers stay at sea for weeks at a time. They have large nets that catch lots of fish in one go.

who's this?

Going down...

Sailors and scientists use special vehicles to travel under water... all the way to the bottom. Gulp!

Scientists use research ships to find out what's happening under the sea. They make maps of the sea-bed and study how water moves around the oceans.

Research ships can drill right down into the sea-bed and bring up things they find there!

what's down there?

A submarine is a boat that can stay underwater for a long time. It is like a floating corridor that can dive to the bottom of the sea and stay there – for up to six months at a time.

Down below

Submarines can be tiny or very big. Around 150 people can live and work on board a large submarine.

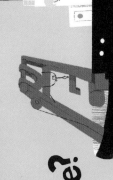

i'm a sperm whale

i'm a sperm whale
and i like to eat
giant squid!

Yikes!

HELLO!

Small vehicles called submersibles
are lowered from research ships.
The scientists on board explore the
sea-bed for a few hours at a time.

The deeper you go under the
sea, the more pressure there
is and the darker it is!

Submersibles send back
pictures of the bottom
of the sea and of the
amazing creatures that
live there.

Wow!

Challenger is a submersible
that went to the Marianas
Trench, the deepest part of
the ocean anywhere on Earth.
It lies 11 kilometres down at
the bottom of the
Pacific Ocean.

Fly like a bird

We may not have wings, but that hasn't stopped people from building amazing vehicles to fly in the skies above us.

Up, up and away!

The Montgolfier brothers were the first people to reach the sky. They launched their hot-air balloon in 1783. Their passengers were a duck, a cockerel, and a sheep!

Nothing flies better than me!

Buckle up and get ready for take-off.

Wow!

Orville and Wilbur Wright were brothers who invented the aeroplane. They made their first flight in 1903 in the USA. The flight only lasted about 12 seconds!

An aeroplane has big, fixed wings and huge engines. It must move very fast so that air passes over the wings and lifts the plane.

**BOOOOM!
ZOOOOM!**

The Boom Supersonic is a new plane that will start flying in 2025. It will travel at 2335 kilometres per hour – faster than the speed of sound!

At any moment, there are at least 5000 planes in the sky, carrying about eight million people around the world every day!

Wow!

In Italy, about 500 years ago, a famous painter and all-round genius called Leonardo da Vinci drew sketches of a flying machine. Modern helicopters come from his amazing idea.

Helicopters are small and nippy! Instead of wings, they have thin blades that spin so fast they push air down, which forces the helicopter up!

I can fly straight up, or down, and hover!

Out of this world

We can now travel beyond the clouds
all the way to outer space – in a rocket!

what's the quickest way to the Moon?
In a great, big rocket!

The space module at
the top is where the
astronauts sit.

Small spacecraft for
exploring the Moon and
planets are stored here.

These boosters
provide the power to
push the spacecraft
to the Moon.

Fastest

The United States is building
a new rocket, called a Space
Launch System, or SLS, to
take astronauts to the Moon!
It will be the most powerful
space rocket – and
the fastest vehicle –
ever built!

Astronauts have already flown to the Moon.
In fact, they've even been to the other side
of the Moon, which is more than 400,000
kilometres from Earth.

This tank holds the rocket's fuel.

5, 4, 3, 2, 1 ...

we have Lift-off!

Powerful rocket boosters launch the rocket.

Here are the engines.

Wow!

The *Apollo 11* space mission was the first to land on the Moon. In 1969, the space rocket carried three American astronauts to the Moon. Two of the astronauts walked on the Moon's surface.

Curiosity is the name of a vehicle exploring the planet Mars right now! It has been on the red planet for years, searching for water, testing rocks and taking pictures, then sending the results and pictures back to Earth!

Globe trotting

All over the world, people use weird and wonderful vehicles to move around.

The Hong Kong junk is a kind of Chinese boat has been around for thousands of years. It's fast and easy to control, and is still used in Hong Kong to sail between the city's 260 islands!

I'm a Hong Kong junk! Check out my sails!

Wow!

Melbourne, in Australia, has more trams than any other city in the world. Over 400 trams criss-cross the city keeping everyone moving!

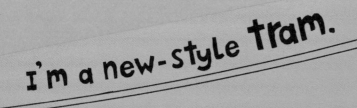

I'm a new-style tram.

Is it a train? Is it a bus? No, it's a tram! A tram runs along tracks on the ground called tramways. There are trams in heaps of cities all over the world, carrying millions of passengers every day!

A cable car is a vehicle that is pulled along by a network of super-strong metal cables. From North and South America, to China, Vietnam and Europe, cable cars are used more and more often to transport people.

Going up!

Tuk tuk, tuk tuk, tuk tuk

This buzzy little three-wheeled taxi is called an auto-rickshaw. It zips in and out of traffic in busy Asian cities. It's called a tuk-tuk in Thailand because of the sound it makes!

29

Into the future

What kind of vehicle do you think you will use in the future? A flying car maybe?

It's possible that one day we may have flying cars that look something like this. But it won't be soon. How would you control thousands of cars in the sky above a city?

IS it a car or is it a plane?

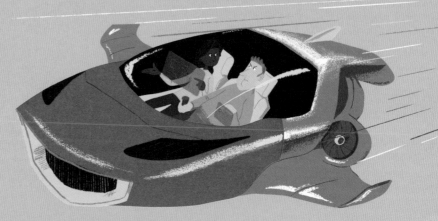

Wow!

Cars that can drive themselves are not a thing of the future. We have them already! You can hop in a Waymo driverless taxi in some cities in the USA. Soon, driverless cars might be in your town or city too!

Invisible light beams, called lasers, build up a very real picture of everything around the car.

Eight cameras on the car tell the car where it is.

The driverless car has a complex computer system.

Radar sensors can tell if there are objects close by, even in rain, snow and fog.

Look, no hands!

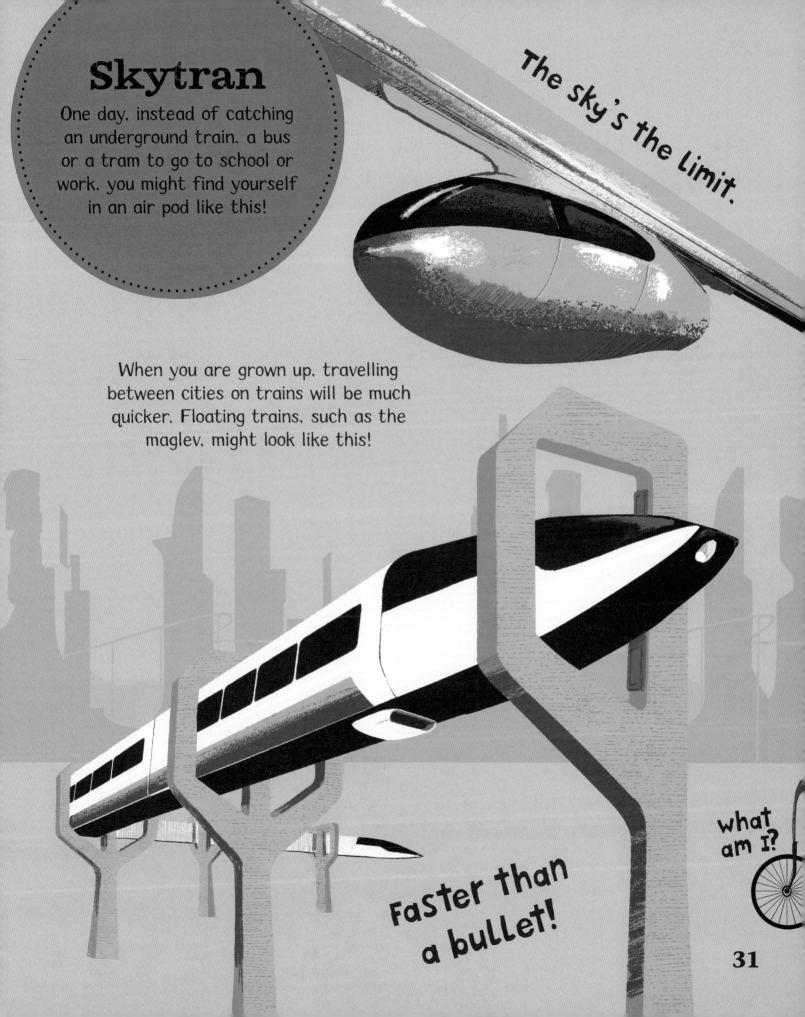

Skytran

One day, instead of catching an underground train, a bus or a tram to go to school or work, you might find yourself in an air pod like this!

When you are grown up, travelling between cities on trains will be much quicker. Floating trains, such as the maglev, might look like this!

Faster than a bullet!

what am I?

31

Wacky races

Not all vehicles are built to be practical. Some people have crazy ideas!

If Leonardo da Vinci's flying machine had been built, it would have looked like this. Crazy or what?

Is it a bird?

Toot, toot!

This nippy car is called a Messerschmitt. It was built in a German aeroplane factory until 1964 and it only had three wheels!

More than 100 years ago, the first vehicle to be called a bicycle was invented. It was called the penny farthing. Imagine riding around the park on that!

I'm a penny farthing!

Is it a car or a house?

Fancy a ride in the Neverwas Haul House? This handmade vehicle is three storeys high and made mostly from recycled materials. It has a top speed of 8 kilometres per hour!